| Table of Content

Chapter 1 – Planning – be patient

- 180 day waiting period
- Veteran's preference
- Veteran's Administration (VA) Disability Rating
- Email, Access, and Dual Factor Authentication
- Intro to USA jobs

Chapter 2 – Applying – be informed

- USA Jobs Specific Resume
- References
- USA Jobs Search function and automatic emails
- Veteran's Hiring Council and Agency specific points of contact

Chapter 3 – The Hiring Process – Don't Quit Your Day Job

- Notional timelines
- Direct Hire Authority

Chapter 4 – Receipt of your Tentative Job Offer (TJO)

- What to check/verify on your TJO
- Tentative Job Offer – example TJO

Chapter 5 – Maintaining your options

- Exceptional qualifications (request for salary match) – example memo
- Enhanced Leave considerations – example memo
- Disabled Veterans' Leave
- Relocation Incentives
- Property and Real Estate Fees

Foreword

This book is a compilation of the recommendations and lessons learned (with links to source documentation) that I discovered throughout more than a year of actively working and wading through the federal government's hiring process. This is my attempt to capture and share the experiences and lessons that I have identified throughout this process, so that you can learn and benefit from them.

This ebook reflects my experience, "the gouge" as we say, or the inside info that I would share with you over lunch.

Introduction

My intent in writing this ebook is to save you time and hassle, by condensing all of the various parts of the hiring processes which are of specific interest and value to veterans, in order to allow you to maximize your benefits when joining the civil service. I have found a lot of people assume that you will know some (or all) of this info, and yet, it's not written down or codified anywhere. Well, until now.

This ebook is intended to be an action guide to walk you through the federal hiring process, to ensure that you don't inadvertently: make mistakes; leave anything on the table; or neglect to request some entitlement at the right point in the process. At the end of the ebook there is an action checklist, broken down by chapter. Follow this and you should remain on-track!

If you have questions, concerns or recommendations, you can feel free to email me at: adtogs2021@gmail.com - that's "ADtoGS" or "Active Duty to Government Service" and also the hashtag (#ADtoGS) that I hope you will use during future discussions on Linked In, where we can share additional insights with the wider community. Good luck!

Chapter 1

"Be patient."

If you're planning to retire from Active duty and join the ranks of our civilian counterparts, the most importance rule to follow is: be patient! This is especially relevant during this time of COVID and its enduring impacts on the workforce, where many more people are working from home or in opposite teams which may contribute to additional delays.

While it may seem like a natural transition there are many reasons why joining the federal civil service is not as easy and seamless as you may expect.

First, under Section 3326 of United States Code Title 5, there is a 180-day waiting period, before a retired member of the armed forces can be appointed into the federal civil service - within DoD. If you're applying to another agency within the federal government, this restriction should not apply. Now, you may know many "other guys" who transitioned directly uniform to civilian service; but, that was only allowed under the waiver of this law, following Sept. 11, 2001, when a national emergency was declared. The law and associated waiting period, was reinstated in 2017. (Among many other lines of activity, MOAA is working to repeal this[1].)

That doesn't mean that it's impossible to obtain civilian employment with DoD within 180 days of retiring, as waivers may be allowed under certain circumstances, but they may not be well-known (or fully understood) by the computer algorithms and/or the Human Resources (HR) staff that handle your application. If you think you qualify for a waiver or exception to policy, you may need to call that out specifically in your application and cover letter. You should reach out to the HR Point of Contact as well, listed near the end of the Vacancy Announcement on USA Jobs.

Second, it's just not that easy… The USG (and specifically DoD) civilian Human Resources (HR) process is deliberately linear and methodical. It has been intentionally made that way to prevent inappropriate influences. So, if you're interested in joining the civil service you need to become familiar with the rules that apply specifically to you and the position(s) that you are seeking.

---

1. Help MOAA End the '180-Day Rule' for Retirees Seeking Most DoD Civilian Jobs, by Mark Belinsky June 1, 2020. https://www.moaa.org/content/publications-and-media/news-articles/2020-news-articles/advocacy/help-moaa-end-the-180-day-rule-for-retirees-seeking-most-dod-civilian-jobs/

The most common entry into the federal civil service is via an appointment to the competitive service, and a job announcement advertised on USA Jobs. This is the traditional route to Government Service, what this ebook refers to as "GS" positions. This actually comes from the list of positions on the General Schedule Pay Plan. Some other agencies have different Pay Plans and associated codes (eg., NH for the acquisition workforce). They are listed here: https://www.opm.gov/policy-data-oversight/pay-leave/pay-administration/fact-sheets/pay-plans/.

Some positions will be advertised as "Open to the Public" while others may be limited to a more specific group, such as "Current Federal Employees." However, as a veteran, you may be entitled to Veteran's Preference, which allows you to apply to many, if not all, open vacancies.

The Department of Labor's Veterans' Preference Advisor website provides guidance based upon your particular service at: https://webapps.dol.gov/elaws/vets/vetpref/mservice.htm. This website will help you determine which, if any, preference you are entitled to receive based upon your service.

It may come as a surprise to many of you, that if you're an officer retiring with a pension (O-4 and above) you may not be entitled to any preference whatsoever.

There are exceptions to this, such as having served during specific periods and/or campaigns.

It may also surprise you to learn that there are three types of Veteran's preference:

1. **Sole Survivorship** (0 point preference eligible), being the only surviving child in a family in which the father or mother or sibling died while on active duty;

2. **Non-Disabled** (5 point preference eligible), if your active duty service was during a war, campaign or expedition for which a campaign medal or badge has been authorized. Largely for this audience, you would have served more than 180 consecutive days (other than for training) from September 11, 2001, and ending on August 31, 2010, the last day of Operation Iraqi Freedom, or During the Gulf War, between August 2, 1990 and January 2, 1992.

3. **Disabled** (10 point preference eligible), this preference is determined and granted by the Veteran's Administration.

See https://www.fedshirevets.gov/job-seekers/veterans/veterans-preference/ for more detail.

The Department of Veteran's Affairs (VA) is the sole authority for determining the 10-point Veteran's preference. This is granted if you are deemed to have a service-connected disability, greater than 30%.

In order to determine your status with the Veteran's Administration, you need to be prepared. For starters, even if you're in perfect health (and I truly hope that you are!) you should file your medical record and application for disability with the VA, immediately. This process may be started prior to separation but should be completed immediately upon separation or retirement. This will allow the VA time to process your records and inform you of their findings, as soon as possible. In January 2021, the VA advertised their average number of days to complete disability-related claims as 154 days.

All the major service affiliated organizations (i.e., VFW, DAV, etc.) will assist you in filing this paperwork and they are excellent resources for navigating the VA process. There is no need to pay anyone else to do this for you.

The VA provides a wealth of information on their website, including how to apply, here: https://www.va.gov/disability/. You will likely be asked to conduct a few in-person physicals, at the VA or their other providers in your area. You must complete these for the VA to have the necessary information to complete your claim. (Hint: This is not the time to be shy about telling and showing every ache, pain, limited mobility or scar. In my case, I had previously broken my neck and had major surgery with retained hardware, for which I was given a 10% disability, but the tiny scar from that same surgery added another 5%. Don't withhold anything, ensure the VA has all the information and documentation necessary to make their determination.)

A few months later, you'll learn the results of your VA eligibility for: covered medical conditions; hiring preference; and may even receive tax-free financial compensation (Disability Compensation). **(Hint: If you don't want the VA's tax-free money for life, consider that they're paying you because they calculate your life expectancy and/or your quality of life may be reduced.)** When you receive your determination letter, they'll even tell you how to appeal their finding, if you're unhappy with the outcome. I found the VA to be the most straightforward aspect of my retirement and transition.

A brief on note what Veteran's Preference means. Normally, Human Resources will assign a numerical score to each application received, in order to determine which resumes and cover letters will be forwarded to the hiring manager for consideration, often referred to as the "certification list." Receiving your veteran's preference (0, 5 or 10 points) will only assist in boosting your score to make "the cert" (as it's commonly referred to) and give the hiring manager an opportunity to elect to interview you. Veteran's Preference does not guarantee that you will get the job, or even "make the cert." You must be found 'highly qualified' by the HR staff, who review only the information contained in your specific application, in order to be passed onto the hiring manager for further consideration.

OPM provides veteran's preference guidance for HR professionals, here: https://www.opm.gov/policy-data-oversight/veterans-services/vet-guide-for-hr-professionals/

As you're waiting for the VA's finding, the best place to spend your time in on the USAJobs.com website. The US Government offers on-line tutorials and even has some helpful videos on You-tube. Many service organizations also offer some helpful introductory seminars, but, like many things in life, experience is everything, so start looking on USA Jobs, today!

USA Jobs and US Government Human Resource personnel rely almost exclusively on email for communication. This is especially true during the COVID epidemic of 2020-2021, with many of Human Resources personnel working from home. But I can't overemphasize this enough, your email connectivity will be critical to your success in finding a position in the civil service. When you start your account on USA Jobs. Do NOT use your current employer's email or phone number. Ensure that your point of contact information (as listed in your account info and on your resume) is correct and that these means of communication will remain current and accessible to you in a few months (up to a year's time.) Do NOT establish your USA Jobs account with your CAC card and active duty email, as you will lose both upon retirement.

Allow me to provide a brief example. A good friend updated her USA Jobs profile and resume while assigned abroad, working at the U.S. Embassy, using her state.gov email address and her state department issued International phone, anticipating a 3 year assignment. However, when the COVID epidemic hit, she was evacuated to the U.S., where she promptly lost access to both her State issued email and phone. It required significant effort for her to delete her old USA Jobs account and re-create a new one through Login.gov – all while a tentative job offer was pending!

Establish all of your retirement, transition and job-seeking accounts with the following:

1. a professional sounding email address from a trusted provider (Hint: nothing like, DJ_JazzyJeff69@eros.com). Gmail is the standard; (Hint: if you don't want to attract attention to your age, don't use an outdated provider, like AOL.)

2. an email that you can easily access (again Gmail, with access from your phone);

3. a reliable (cell/mobile) phone number that you can access anywhere, especially when dual factor authorization (receipt of text message) is required by most USG websites, such as USA Jobs and the VA.

One of the key challenges will be the creation of your USA Jobs federal resume – a real beast! Unlike resumes in the "real" world these USA Jobs resumes often comprise ten or more pages, detailing everything you have done and accomplished throughout your military career, or at a minimum for the past ten years. I recommend Kathryn Troutman's *Federal Resume Guidebook*. As her book attests, this level of detail is helpful, or even necessary, for the word-search algorithms which match your qualifications to the position description and allow you to progress in the hiring process. (As a gauge, my printed federal resume runs 12 pages.)

As with most things in life, you will learn so much more by doing… you will learn which documents are required (DD-214, school transcripts, etc.); what format they should be in for up-loading (.pdf); how to properly name them (no special characters) and which files will be retained for future applications. So, take some time and go through the process of applying for a position on USA Jobs, today. Just walking through the steps of applying for a position – any position – will be educational for you.

Some of you may be asking: "If there's a 180-day waiting period, why would I apply for a job now?" The real point in doing this now, is to prepare yourself and to gain familiarization with the process, so that you will be ready. If your experience is anything like mine, you're likely to discover that your dream job is seeking applicants; however, you'll learn this at about 10 pm, and that the application window closes at midnight. But if you follow the advice here, you'll be ready!

Chapter 2

"Be informed."

At this point, you should have prepared yourself by creating an account on USA Jobs website, and walked yourself through the application process on at least one position. If you haven't already discovered this, USA Jobs has a special webpage for veterans, available here: https://www.usajobs.gov/Help/working-in-government/unique-hiring-paths/veterans/

Another useful tool is the Feds Hire Vet's website, at: https://www.fedshirevets.gov/

Hopefully, after taking the advice in Chapter #1, you will have already applied for a job, just to understand the process and documents required. In order to do so, you would have built your USA Jobs Resume and saved it to your profile (have I mentioned Kathryn Troutman's book and reminded you to spell-check?). There are some great step-by-step instructions here: https://www.usajobs.gov/Help/how-to/account/documents/resume/build/ and information on what to include (or perhaps exclude, such as experience greater than 10 years old) here: https://www.usajobs.gov/help/faq/application/documents/resume/what-to-include/

You should also upload other important documents which will be required to complete almost any application on USA Jobs, such as: transcripts, DD-214, VA eligibility letter (if you have it already – if not a placeholder letter from you, stating when you expect to receive it, may suffice) and perhaps, most importantly, your SF-15, the official paperwork required to declare your veteran's preference. It is available, here: https://www.opm.gov/forms/pdf_fill/sf15.pdf. Pay particular attention to the instructions and requirements for different supporting documentation, such as the DD-214. (Hint: I recommend you include any/all supporting documentation in a single file that you scan and upload titled "LAST NAME SF-15".)

Now, we just need to find the "right job" to apply to and you'll be a few clicks away from applying!

Finding the "right job" on USA Jobs… hmmm. The easiest and best way, is when a former boss or colleague emails you a link and says, "We think you'd be perfect for this position, we sure would like you to apply!" That's certainly one of the best ways to find an opportunity in the civil service. They recognize the skills they require and having worked with you previously, they know what you have to offer. It tells you that you're pushing on an open door and this anecdote serves as great reminder of the importance of networking, both in-person and on-line. If you're not actively doing this, it's time to start. This article provides some insight: https://www.military.com/veteran-jobs/career-advice/military-transition/networking-strategy-for-transition.html

The next best way of finding the right job is to have USA Jobs email them to you. Yeah, no kidding, the website will send you daily/weekly/monthly emails with jobs that match your criteria. It's a fantastic tool – but, like all tools, you need to learn how to use it properly. First, you'll need to search for the exact type (or types) of jobs you're interested in and learn the key words for those positions. If you know the exact position you're after, reach out to whoever is in that position now, and enquire as to the job's exact title and Job Series. Once you've searched for that title, try it again with a new location or pay grade. And if you've found a position that interests you, scroll almost to the bottom and click on the Job Series to see other similar positions. (Hint: when looking through these positions, the unique words and phrases listed as requirements should be very similar to the phrases used in your resume!) When you find positions that you like (even if you have no plan to actually apply) you can click on the yellow star and save that position for future reference.

I had several generic searches set up, some by profession, some by location and they would send me an email once a week, (if you set it up on a Tuesday, reminder emails will be sent every Tuesday), listing all available openings. And I do mean ALL. (As interested as I am in aviation and helicopters, I am not likely to apply for a fire fighting job that requires jumping out of a helicopter, for $11/hour!) So, trust me when I say, it takes some time to learn to use all of the filters and options available in order to narrow your search results so that they are actually relevant and meaningful to you (in my example, I then added a salary filter).

Setting up your own automatic search function is the most reliable way to discover your future position; not every former boss or colleague will reach out to inform you about the next opening. Some may be looking to promote from within, and many just won't remember to think of you when the position posts (remembering you have a 180-day cooling off period before you can be re-hired in DoD). And, they're working and busy, right?

Let the automation work for you. Start here: https://www.usajobs.gov/Help/how-to/search/ and become familiar with the search function and the many filters available to you, here: https://www.usajobs.gov/Help/how-to/search/filters/

A weekly email from USA Jobs has been more than sufficient for me, but when you receive the email, pay immediate and close attention to the "open period" for applications – especially if you're overseas, traveling or crossing multiple time zones. If you've set up a search for "THE" job you're after, you may elect daily notifications, as some positions are only advertised for a brief period (i.e., 72 hours).

You need to keep informed of any changes to the US Government hiring policies, practices or procedures, particularly if they apply to you or your anticipated career field. During COVID, many positions were granted exceptions and exemptions for expedited hiring, particularly, healthcare positions supporting Operation "Warp Speed."

It's best to spend some time on USA Jobs and the Office of Personnel Management (OPM) websites and their Social Media platforms (i.e., Facebook and/or Twitter) for the very latest news, which may impact you or affect your hiring status.

This seems an appropriate time to discuss your preparation, specifically regarding your own social media presence. In today's job-hunting environment it is extremely important to maintain an up-to-date and professional Linked In profile. The time and effort you spend on Linked In will be extremely helpful for your networking efforts as well, re-connecting with friends and former colleagues who may tip you off to potential opportunities. It's common practice for HR staff or personnel on your interview and hiring panels to have researched the candidates prior to your interview. (Hint: You need to 'google yourself.' What does your social media presence on Facebook, Instagram and Linked In say about you? If there is anything negative, you may want - or need - to address it.)

Each of the federal agencies maintains a Veterans Employment Program Office, which may be helpful to you if/when you are applying for positions within certain agencies. The Veteran's Hiring Council representative is usually a veteran at that specific Agency who has been tasked to serve as an internal advocate for hiring veterans. You may never actually engage with them, unless there is an issue, but they should be engaged internally, on your behalf. As an example, when I was seeking employment with USAID, I copied the Veteran's Hiring Council point of contact on all of my correspondence.

The complete list of points of contact is available here: https://www.fedshirevets.gov/veterans-council/agency-directory/.

Each vacancy announcement on USA Jobs is organized into the following 7 sections:

1. **Overview** – salary, pay grade, closing date, appointment type and service;

2. **Location(s)** – some jobs have multiple vacancies and locations, pay attention to any relocation expenses which may be authorized;

3. **Duties** – you should understand the particular responsibilities mentioned, whether you will supervise others and any potential for promotion;

4. **Requirements** – perhaps the most important section citizenship and security clearance particulars; knowledge, skills and abilities, "How you will be evaluated" and "Job Questionnaire";

5. **Required documents** – ensure you have these ready to upload when you submit your application (or a placeholder, explaining when you expect it; such as your VA disability determination);

6. **Benefits** – ensure you understand how these contribute to the expected total compensation offered for this position;

7. **How to apply** – application steps and what's next after submitting your application.

In the upper right corner of each section on USA Jobs, there is a question mark icon which will take you to the help section – it's very useful! But allow me to provide some additional information on some the particulars mentioned above.

The Federal Government consists of three types of services: Competitive Service, Excepted Service, and the Senior Executive Service.

The Competitive Service consists of all civil service positions in the executive branch of the Federal Government with some exceptions. In the competitive service, individuals must go through a competitive hiring process (i.e., competitive examining) before being appointed to a position, generally open to all applicants. This may consist of an evaluation of the individual's education and experience, and/or a written exam or test.

Appointments in the Excepted Service are civil service appointments within the Federal Government that <u>do not</u> confer competitive status and they may have certain limitations, such as length of service and/or promotion potential.

The Senior Executive Service (SES) (not discussed in this ebook) is the cohort of men and women charged with transforming and leading the federal government. These Flag-Officer equivalent personnel have been specifically promoted for their leadership qualities.

More detailed information on the different types of service can be found at: https://www.opm.gov/policy-data-oversight/hiring-information/hiring-authorities/

The Requirements section contains some of the most important and helpful information for your application.

- Pay particular attention to the Security Clearance requirement. Is it required as a prerequisite to apply? This is usually listed as "must currently possess." Or is it required prior to employment? This is listed as "must be eligible to attain." The exact wording matters for your eligibility. While this will be a common refrain throughout this ebook, it bares stating here: the security clearance may be the longest part of your hiring process.

- Your resume should clearly demonstrate your level of familiarity with the knowledge, skills and abilities listed ("KSAs" in HR lingo). The KSAs will be graded based upon the categories listed in the "how you will be evaluated" section. (Hint: I suggest you modify your resume to specifically address the KSAs and evaluation categories.)

- The Job Questionnaire is essentially a self-test. It allows the HR Staff to rapidly evaluate and group candidates based upon their own answers to the questions. (Hint: Always preview the Job Questionnaire before applying. If you're not able to answer most/all of these questions with the highest category response, you may not be well suited for this position.)

- Finally, when you submit your information to the agency ensure all of your application (and files) transfer across. USA Jobs will automatically take you to the applicable website, just don't be too surprised if you need to upload and re-submit documents.

For your resume, I highly recommend you buy (or borrow from your local library) Kathryn Troutman's *Federal Resume Guidebook*. It is, in my opinion, THE best resource available for veteran's writing or revising their USA Jobs resume. Additionally, her other book, *The Stars are Lined Up for Military Spouses for Federal Careers*, is also an excellent source with step-by-step instructions that are equally relevant to veterans.

In preparation for your interview(s), my advice is limited. Again, I refer you elsewhere for true subject matter expertise: buy (or borrow) Lin Grensing-Pophal's, *The Everything Job Interview Book*, or almost any of the books on the market and read through cover to cover. You should know as much as possible about the organization that you are applying to.

I suggest that you do your research and think like a reporter:

- Who are the key players, from CEO to current director and your hiring panel? (Hint: they will have researched you on Linked In and Google. Have you done the same?)

- What is the mission of this organization, and specifically your prospective role in it?

- Where are they located, both physically and within the larger organization? Are you expected to: work from home, travel, or deploy? Where do you fit within the broader organization?

- Why are they filing this vacancy at this time?

- How does the organization contribute to the overall mission/national policy objectives?

Some of the most common and/or most challenging interview questions are scenario based, for example, "Tell us about a time when you…". I suggest that you prepare a few answers (say 6 or 10 of them) in the STAR format: Situation, Task, Action, Result. The scenarios that you choose to describe should be pivotal memories etched into your mind after years of service, where you can clearly and succinctly: describe the situation you encountered, the tasking you received, the action you decided to take (and why) and the result you/your team achieved; including any metrics which you developed or used in order to measure your success.

These STAR scenarios that you chose as examples should be pivotal events which you can re-live and re-tell, as clearly as if they occurred yesterday. Especially now, with the benefit of hindsight, you will likely have drawn more than one lesson from them. Therefore, more often than not, you'll be able to tell the same story, and conclude it differently; allowing you to share the same "sea-story" in the S - T - A format and yet flip the Result, in order to answer different questions.

For example, the story of the time when you had to overhaul the way things had previously been done in order to meet mission, can equally be used as your response when asked, "Tell us about a time when you stepped in to change the process and improve efficiency or save time/money." And, "Tell us a time when you and your team created real and meaningful organizational change." Or even, "Tell us a time when you disagreed with your boss or disagreed with the way your organization was conducting business."

It's the same story, but adopted to field the question at-hand. The key is to make sure that you can make your story succinct, and understandable as you deliver a result that is directly related to the interview question being asked. All the while, hammering home the fact that you possess the particular Knowledge, Skills, Abilities and Judgment that this position requires.

Then, have a friend (not your spouse/significant other) conduct at least one practice interview with you. Don't use acronyms - and don't curse. Ask them to critique you - with brutal honestly (that's' why I suggested NOT using your spouse in this role.) They can even video you, so you can critique yourself later. This is especially important in the age of COVID, with our reliance upon Zoom and Microsoft Teams. You may come across differently using these media. (Hint: you should be familiar with these IT tools prior to your first interview.)

Now, practice until *nearly* perfect, you don't want your answers to come across as *too* scripted, and you'll be ready!

Chapter 3
"Don't Quit Your Day Job"

In this section we're going to discuss the timeline for the hiring process with a reminder: don't quit your current job! It may take up to a <u>year</u> to get hired.

The official explanation of the hiring process for positions in the Civil Service is provided a here: https://www.usajobs.gov/Help/faq/application/process/.

For veteran's reading this, your process should run like this:

Planning	Applying	Up to TJO	TJO - FJO	FJO - Joining
Verify veteran's preference using Dept of Labor website	Create your federal resume, using Ms. Troutman's book	Rehearse 6-8 scenario based S-T-A-R Formats	Re-read and verify your TJO	Complete urinalysis: keep paperwork & email HRO
Apply for disability from Veteran's Administration	Complete your SF-15 for Veteran's Preference	Conduct at least 1 practice interview in-person	Communicate questions or concerns - immediately	Complete physical exam
Create a USA Jobs account – walk through job application	Upload required documents to USA Jobs profile	Ensure you're familiar with Zoom and Microsoft teams	Respond before deadline	Update Security Clearance using e-Qip, save a copy
Verify your email and mobile phone will meet requirements	Set up USA Jobs search(es)		Keep your options open – seek other employment	Submit fingerprints
	Update your Social Media profile, Facebook and Linked In (Google yourself)		Submit memorandum for: "Superior Qualifications" "Enhanced Leave" and Disabled Veteran's Leave	Re-read & verify FJO
	Identify Veteran's Hiring Council Representative for desired agencies		Submit request for any relocation incentive(s)	Communicate concerns - immediately
				Respond by deadline

Priorities:
1) VA paperwork
2) USA Jobs education
3) Networking

Priorities:
1) Keeping all options open!
2) Pursuing other job(s) that you desire
3) Refining your resume
4) Honing interview skills

Priorities :
1) Understanding the Civil Service
2) Maximizing your benefits
3) Preparing for a move & new career

Note, the above process should begin well before your retirement, and you should certainly be active (and hopefully also otherwise employed) throughout your 180 waiting-period. I have not discovered any rule that says that you can't 'apply' for jobs during this time; but frankly, if you've applied to the VA, I suggest that you wait until you have your disability determination, as it carries significant weight with the HR staff; especially if you're rated above 30% disabled.

From my experience, the process, from application to reporting, has run more like this:

Position Advertised	Initial HR Process	CERT for Highly Qualified	Identify for Interview	Interview Ranking Select	HR Checks Ref's	TJO Issued	Urinalysis Physical Fingerprint Security clearance	FJO Issued	Orders Issued	Report Date Assigned
New positions may take up to 12 months to create, fund, approve and post to USA jobs. Positions advertised 3-7 days, max 14 days.	HR determine initial quals. HR updates CERT list. USA Jobs updated.	Only 'highly qualified' applicants passed on to hiring manager for review.	Hiring manager assembles selection & interview panel.	Scheduling and holidays (for panel and candidates) may extend this period.	Ensure your Reference POC info is up-to-date!	Congrats! Don't quit your day job!	These tasks are your responsibility to schedule & complete.	Last chance for any requests, negotiations, or changes.	Ensure any dependents & allowances are included.	Usually the start of a Pay Period (every 2 weeks). Be ready for TSP, FEGLI and FEHP decisions.

Each step should take less than 2 weeks, for a total of 22 weeks or about 4-5 months, based upon my experience. While my experience may be a unique case, it still takes longer than you may expect. According to Govexec.com, "Agencies on average have improved the time it takes to hire new employees in recent years: in fiscal 2018, the hiring process took 98.3 days, compared with 105.8 days in fiscal 2017."[2]

Okay, but that would only account for 3-4 months, why did you say that it may take a year?

Well, the reality is that your security clearance alone could take up to a year. My security clearance took 6 months and was described by several involved as 'remarkably quick'.

Additionally, if the position that you're offered happens to be overseas (such as my case), you will need to add the following requirements to your timeline, which can only be accomplished in series, after receipt of your orders:

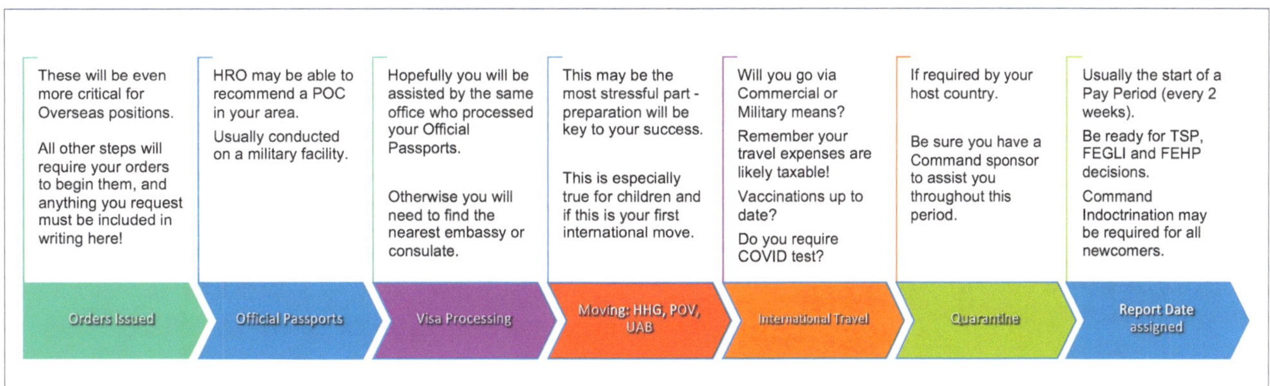

---

2. Wagner, Erich. "OPM Announces Adjustments to Annual Time-to-Hire Metrics." FEBRUARY 26, 2020. https://www.govexec.com/management/2020/02/opm-announces-adjustments-annual-time-hire-metrics/163361/

Again, each step should take about 2 weeks, for a total of 14 weeks, or another 2-3 months. This is based upon my recent experience and research. One recent example, shared by an Army veteran and civil servant helps illustrate this point: "It took 4 months from advertising to on-boarding for a new employee. He/she was: a) an existing civil servant; b) working for the same federal agency; c) had the correct clearance, and; d) moved from another command, located on the very same installation!"

Your experience may differ, and will be dependent upon many factors, some outside of your control: such as, the speed of processing for Official Passports and visas.

Other factors which are within your control are:

- Your paperwork: original birth certificates, marriage licenses and car titles are required;

- Your licensing: valid personal passports, and re-newed driver's licenses;

- Your physical preparedness for an overseas move: figuratively and literally you need to get your house in order, now, for your HHG, UAB and POV shipments.

The Federal Government is well aware that the hiring process is lengthy and potentially flawed:

The Federal hiring process has long been criticized for being lengthy, not resulting in qualified candidates, and being too complex for applicants and even hiring officials to understand. Many reform efforts have centered on improving the hiring process, but criticisms continue. To address perceived inefficiencies in Federal hiring, the Government has created a number of sanctioned alternatives to the competitive hiring process. One of these alternatives is the direct hire authority, which streamlines some competitive hiring procedures." [3]

---

3. U.S. Merit Systems Protection Board Office of Policy and Evaluation, Research Brief, Feb 2021 https://www.mspb.gov/MSPBSEARCH/viewdocs.aspx?docnumber=1803830%20&version=1810102&application=ACROBAT

For a list of the agencies and job series that OPM has granted Direct Hire Authority, check here: https://www.opm.gov/policy-data-oversight/hiring-information/direct-hire-authority/#url=Governmentwide-Authority. (Usually, hard to fill medical, legal and IT positions.)

Stick with it, the US Government does hire people everyday (well actually, only every two-weeks at the start of each pay period). It just takes patience. And don't quit your current job until you have been assigned an actual start date!

Chapter 4

"Receipt of your Tentative Job Offer."

Let's assume that you've made it this far… and you've been offered a position: Congratulations! This is called a "Tentative Job Offer" or TJO for short.

First, it's important to emphasize the "Tentative" nature of this offer.

The hiring agency can withdraw their offer for almost any reason. Despite what you may feel at the time, some legitimate reasons exist for cancelling positions that have <u>nothing</u> to do with you. Seriously. I'm referring to enterprise-wide changes/concerns such as budget constraints, furloughs, agency or government wide hiring freeze, etc.

They can also cancel the tentative offer for issues that they may discover relating to you, specifically; any negative information disclosed by your references or during your background/security clearance process. Should the agency withdraw or cancel its TJO, I don't believe they have any obligation to disclose their reasoning. But I certainly hope that won't be the case for you!

Now that we've discussed the possible negative outcomes of your Tentative Job Offer, let's focus on the positive aspects and your options/actions required. Upon receipt of your TJO (see example page 23), you'll once again be directed to the USA Jobs onboarding website to accept the offer. However, before doing so, be sure to thoroughly re-read it in its entirety. If there is anything mentioned that you don't understand completely, look it up on OPM.gov; and if you still have reservations, contact your servicing Human Resources Office (HRO), listed in the TJO.

Specifically, you will want to focus on and ensure you agree with:

1. **The position title** – it may sound petty, but ensure this is the exact position that you have applied for. Sometimes, there are slight difference in titles (i.e., "Specialist" versus "Analyst"). This is particularly relevant if the solicitation included several different pay grades, such as GS-9/10/11. (As a side note, once hired you may be re-assigned as the mission dictates, so don't get too wrapped up in positions and titles, just yet.)

2. **The deadline for accepting/declining the position.** DO NOT MISS THIS DEADLINE.

3. **The starting Pay Grade, Step and Salary –** be sure that you are being offered the correct Grade and Step. (Later we will discuss a possible request for "Superior Qualifications.")

4. **The expected tour length –** especially important for overseas positions and managing travel requirements.

5. **The appointment type –** important to note any Probationary/Trial period. Although this is usually not negotiable, you still need to understand what it means. You are essentially a "trial" employee who can be dismissed more easily and you may have limited appeal rights during this period. If you view this initial position as a stepping stone to something greater, you should still be eligible to apply for other federal jobs within your agency during this time, and your probationary period would continue in that new role.

6. **Remember this is the TENTATIVE Job Offer –** don't quit your job or commit any money!

7. **Security Clearance –** verify that the requirement listed matches your current and/or anticipated level of clearance. This is one of the longest tasks to complete prior to hiring and may have the greatest impact on your processing.

8. **Emergency Essential –** this means you may have to stay and work or deploy when others are told to stay at-home or are evacuated.

9. **Travel –** verify the amount of travel matches your expectations. Almost all positions state "some travel required."

10. **PCS Orders and Required Documentation and Travel Arrangements –** be sure you understand these, but don't be overwhelmed, your HRO will assist you. Assuming your position is with DoD, the Defense Financial and Accounting Service (DFAS) provides some great information, here: https://www.dfas.mil/CivilianEmployees/Civilian-Permanent-Change-of-Station-PCS/Understanding-Orders/Traveler/

Once you've verified the above information, proceed to the on-boarding portal where you will be given three options: 1) accept the position; 2) decline the position, or; 3) request additional information. Clearly if you're ready to accept, do so immediately. **I would only recommend that you decline the TJO, if you have already accepted a position elsewhere**.

If so, then decline. Don't wait. If you're somewhere in-between and have questions, doubts or confusion, email your HRO point of contact immediately and click on the "request additional information" option (Hint: I say email, not phone, to ensure your answers are provided in writing.) Either way, ensure that you respond BEFORE the offer expires, usually within 72 hours. (Hint: I recommend that you copy everyone from the hiring manager to the Veteran's Hiring Council representative.)

Example: Tentative Job Offer (TJO) for a notional overseas position

From: HRO Staff at ABC Command
To: (your name/email here)

Subject: Tentative Job Offer For POSITION TITLE, GS-SERIES-## (Announcement ###)

Dear (Your name here),

I am pleased to inform you that you have been tentatively selected for the position of INSERT POSITION TITLE HERE, GS-SERIES-## Step 1 with the Department of the Navy, located at ABC Command. An official job offer will be provided to you once all pre-employment requirements are met.

ACCEPTANCE / DECLINATION OF POSITION: You are required to respond with your acceptance or declination of this tentative job offer, via the link below, no later than (insert date).

INSERT LINK TO USA JOBS ONBOARDING

If you accept this job offer, you will be prompted to sign into our automated onboarding system (using your USAJOBS account) and begin the onboarding process. Failure to respond by the above date may result in you no longer being considered for this position.

A. POSITION OFFER INFORMATION:

1. **Salary:** Your salary will be set at GS-SERIES-## Step 1, $ 98,765.00 per annum. This salary may be adjusted upon receipt of supporting documentation and is not inclusive of any overseas allowances (i.e. Living Quarters Allowance (LQA), Post Allowance (PA), etc.)

2. **Tour of Duty:** The tour of duty for ABC Command is 36 months. However, if you have prior employment affecting tour eligibility the tour length will be adjusted accordingly and stated in your final job offer letter (FJO). [Editor's note: this may differ for CONUS positions]

3. **Appointment Type:** This is a Veterans Employment Opportunity Act (VEOA) with a full-time work schedule. You will be in tenure group II until you complete the two-year probationary period; then you will be changed to tenure group I.

4. **THIS IS A TENTATIVE JOB OFFER.** If you are currently employed, please DO NOT quit your job. DO NOT spend any money or make any life style changes in response to this tentative offer. You will be notified when all conditions have been met and the offer is confirmed. This tentative job offer can be withdrawn at any time during this process pending suitability issues, employment eligibility, physical results, drug testing, etc.).

B. ONBOARDING MANAGER:

The USA Staffing Onboarding Manager System allows candidates to electronically complete and submit the pre-employment forms required to finalize the selection process. You must complete the requested forms in order to come on board without delay. The system will ask you a series of questions, and your answers will be used to fill out the forms automatically. In addition, please complete the attached enclosure attached to this tentative job offer letter and upload them into the system. Please see the attached Overseas Recruitment Guide, page 5 for the Onboarding Manager Checklist.

C. CONDITIONS OF EMPLOYMENT:

This position requires a TOP SECRET clearance. Within a few days from submitting your assigned forms and/or documents, you may receive an email from the servicing Security Office inviting you to complete the electronic Questionnaire for Investigations Processing (e-QIP). Please follow their instructions & complete the e-QIP application within the assigned due date.

If you currently hold the appropriate level of clearance required for this position, an additional request may not be necessary.

This is a drug testing designated position. This tentative job offer is contingent upon successfully completion of a pre-employment drug testing. Once you accept this tentative offer, a drug testing appointment will be coordinated through this Human Resources Office (HRO). A tentative offer of employment will be rescinded if you fail to report to the scheduled drug test appointment. Incumbents of drug testing designated positions will be subject to random testing. Drug test results will be provided to the employing activity/command.

If you are currently in a drug testing position, please provide the name and contact information of your Drug Testing Program Coordinator, an additional request may not be necessary.

This is an Emergency Essential (E-E) position. It is considered essential to support Navy's mobilization and wartime mission. In the event of a crisis situation, the incumbent, must continue to perform the E-E duties until relieved by proper authority. The incumbent maybe required to take part in readiness exercises and to accompany deployed forces. This position cannot be vacated during a national emergency or mobilization without seriously impairing the capability of the organization to function effectively; therefore, the position is designated "key", which requires the incumbent to be exempt from military recall status. Failure to remain in this position & deploy as directed can result in separation for efficiency Federal Service (5 USC 752).

This position might require occasional travel.

Failure to complete the above requirements in a timely manner will delay your pre-employment processing and could result in this offer being withdrawn.

D. FIRM OFFER LETTER AND PERMANENT CHANGE OF DUTY STATION (PCS) ORDERS:

Once all required documents are received and all prerequisite and conditions of employment are met ABC Command will request a firm job offer (FJO) letter from the Office of Civilian Human Resources Stennis (OCHR). Once the FJO has been released and accepted, the HRO benefits team will issue the permanent change of duty station (PCS) orders.

PCS Orders will allow you to request official passports and VISA, arrange shipment for household goods (HHG) and make travel arrangements for you and your family members. Please see the attached Overseas Recruitment Guide, pages 7-8 for additional information on the PCS process.

E. REQUIRED DOCUMENTATION:

PASSPORT: DoD civilian personnel, including dependents, MUST obtain the proper official passport (burgundy color). The official passport establishes the employee as a member of the U.S. Forces serving under the NATO Status of Forces Agreement (SOFA).

VISA: DoD civilian personnel, including dependents, MUST obtain a Visa in their official passport. You cannot enter the country PRIOR to the permission date listed on the VISA. The documents together are the foundation of what permits you and your family members to reside in the host country. The Visa will not be accepted if it is in a tourist passport.

Contact your nearest DoD passport agent to apply for an official passport and VISA. If you are unable to locate a DoD facility, please contact HRO point of contact(s) identified at the end of this TJO for support.

Please see the attached Overseas Recruitment Guide, page 6 for additional information on the required documentation.

F. TRAVEL ARRANGEMENTS:

Upon receipt of the official passport AND Visa for yourself and your eligible family members, the nearest personal property and travel office will assist you with shipment of your household goods (HHG) and your travel arrangements. If you have pets, make sure to discuss travel options directly with the travel office. You will be liable for the cost of the pets. Upon receipt of your travel itinerary, please e-mail a copy to the HRO point of contact(s) identified at the end of this TJO. Please note, traveling from alternate locations or taking leave en route to your new duty stations may impact your entrance on duty date, benefits and allowances.

HOUSEHOLD GOODS (HHG): Contact your Personal Property office to arrange for shipment/storage of your HHG goods. You are eligible to ship/store a total of 18,000 pounds of HHG and Ship one POV (vehicle). If you are going to be leaving some of your HHG-s in non-temporary storage at government expense request the DD Form 1164.

EXCESS BAGGAGE: Travelers should check with individual transportation carriers, prior to travel, about limitations of baggage weight, and/or size, and/or number of bags allowed, and/or waived service charges for accompanied baggage. The traveler should be financially prepared to pay for excess accompanied baggage. Excess baggage reimbursement may be authorized only under unusual circumstances.

Please see the attached Overseas Recruitment Guide, page 8 for additional information on the making travel arrangements.

G. OVERSEAS BENEFITS, ALLOWANCES and ENTITLEMENTS:

Eligibility for overseas allowances (i.e. Living Quarters Allowance (LQA), Separate Maintenance Allowance (SMA), Post Allowance, etc.) will be determined prior to issuance of final job offer.

Please see the attached Overseas Recruitment Guide, pages 9-18 for additional information on overseas allowances, benefits and entitlements.

H. GOVERNMENT ETHICS

Department of the Navy is committed to maintaining an ethical culture and upholding the principles of ethical conduct. As a Department of the Navy employee, you will be subject to the Standards of Ethical Conduct for Employees of the Executive Branch as well as the criminal conflict of interest statutes. If you are a new Government employee, or as a new employee to this Department, you will be required to receive initial ethics orientation within 3 months of appointment. If you have any questions about these requirements, or any government ethics issue, you should contact the ethics counselor for your organization which will be located in your local Counsel or Judge Advocate General's office. If you need assistance locating your local ethics counselor please email ethics@navy.mil <mailto:ethics@navy.mil> .

During this onboarding process, please check your voice messages, email inbox and junk mail folders daily to ensure you receive all your correspondence. Failure to complete the above requirements in a timely manner will delay your pre-employment processing and could result in this offer being withdrawn.

It is imperative that you thoroughly read and review the attached Overseas Recruitment Guide. Please complete the requested forms and upload the required documents in order to proceed and expedite the recruitment process.

The final pages of the guide contain FAQs received by HRO staff. If you have additional questions, contact the HRO POC (listed on the below) if you have additional questions.

Yours sincerely,

HRO Point of Contact

Chapter 5

"Maintain your options."

Contrary to popular belief, you do have some options upon receipt and acceptance of your TJO.

The first - and most important - is to continue to pursue other opportunities, either with the USG or elsewhere. You will want to keep as many irons in the fire as possible, you never know which job offer will come together first. The remaining options we will discuss relate to the position being offered – but keep your current job and keep applying for other positions. As excited as you may be for this new position, keep looking for other opportunities which interest you. You're no longer in the military, and you're not yet a member of the civil service, so you're not committed to anything, yet… take the time to continue to explore what's available to you.

Now, let's concentrate on the position offered in your TJO and your options related to it.

Let's focus on one of the more important aspects, specifically: your **starting salary**. As a veteran transitioning to the civil service, you will be considered as a "newly hired federal employee" and you will be offered your position at the lowest step; i.e., GS-13 Step 1. Upon acceptance of the TJO, this is your time - your ONLY time - to request consideration for a pay raise based upon your **"superior qualifications."** This request may allow HRO to offer you an initial position above Step 1. The Office of Personnel Management lays out 10 criteria (at the link below) which may be considered for establishing the level of your initial pay. Allowable factors include: current/recent salary; your superior skills and competencies; geographical challenges; existing labor markets; disparity between federal and civilian wages; and other relevant factors, spelled out here: https://www.opm.gov/policy-data-oversight/pay-leave/pay-administration/fact-sheets/superior-qualifications-and-special-needs-pay-setting-authority/

In order to request an initial base salary above Step 1 at any paygrade, you must submit a short memo (see example page 32) outlining your case and include any additional justification(s), such as current pay statements, certifications, education or degrees (only those in excess of the minimum required for your position).

Most people will tell you that starting above a Step 1 is impossible; but I will assure that it is not. Originally, I had requested to start as a Step 4 in order to meet my previous salary but I was offered my initial starting salary at Step 3. While this fell just short of my previous salary,

I took it as a "win" and accepted the position. Most local commands only have the flexibility to offer an increase, up to Step 3. Beyond that, it requires review by higher authority, back in D.C. and this would have only further delayed my hiring, ultimately costing more money than it would be worth.

This is a good place to pause and remind you to proceed cautiously and with humility. Any request to start at a salary above that offered (Step 1) must be supported by the Hiring manager and HR Officer; especially, as there are likely to be other short-listed candidates who would accept the position as offered.

As a friend recently said to me, "If you truly think you're GS-15 material, then only apply for GS-15 positions." In other words, don't accept a GS-13 position and try to argue for pay and allowances which would equate to those of a GS-15. It just doesn't work that way. The USG is looking to hire fully qualified individuals at well-known and long-established pay rates.

As a new employee, we need to temper our expectations. The last thing any of us would want is to have our reputation tarnished before we even begin our new career. So, decide which, if any, of these avenues you want to pursue, and balance your request(s) with an ounce of humility, and your expected outcomes with a dose of reality.

Having said that, the second option avail to you is to request consideration for **Enhanced Leave**. In short, you're seeking credit for time served, and you must ask now, or forever hold your peace. The head of an agency, or his or her designee, must make the determination to approve an employee's qualifying prior work experience before the effective date of the employee's entry on duty — **the determination cannot be made retroactively.**

OPM provides guidance here: https://www.opm.gov/policy-data-oversight/pay-leave/leave-administration/fact-sheets/creditable-service-for-annual-leave-accrual-for-non-federal-work-experience-and-experience-in-the-uniformed-service/ and, here: https://www.opm.gov/policy-data-oversight/pay-leave/leave-administration/fact-sheets/annual-leave/

Full time government employees earn leave at the following rates:

Years of Service	Leave earned per pay period (hours)	Leave earned per year (hours)	Leave earned per year (days)
Less than 3	4	104	13
Between 3 - 15	6	156	19.5
Greater than 15	8	208	26

In order to request consideration for Enhanced Leave, you will be asked to complete a Standard Form 144a, which you can find here: https://www.opm.gov/forms/pdf_fill/sf144a.pdf.

Your request (SF-144a) is broken into several parts listing:

A. Creditable Uniformed Service - limited to service in the armed forces during a war or in a campaign or expedition for which a campaign badge has been authorized

B. Creditable Civilian Service - for service under a Federal appointment performing Federal functions under Federal supervision (i.e. possibly government contractor)

C. Creditable Federal Service - former civil service time (this would normally be reflected on an SF-50 from your last position.)

D. Creditable Active Duty Uniformed Service - Active Duty Uniformed Service that otherwise would <u>not</u> be creditable <u>but</u> having duties which directly relate to the duties of the position to which appointed <u>and</u> are necessary to achieve an important agency mission or performance goal.

While the instructions are not very clear for the prospective employee, OPM provides some guidance for servicing Human Resource Offices, here: https://www.opm.gov/policy-data-oversight/data-analysis-documentation/personnel-documentation/servicecreditleave.pdf

When it comes to determining which expeditions and campaigns 'count' for enhanced leave accrual, the list of campaigns eligible for veteran's preference are available, here: https://www.opm.gov/policy-data-oversight/veterans-services/vet-guide-for-hr-professionals/

And lastly, I submitted a memo, just to be sure I covered and explained it all (see example page 33).

I'm not certain exactly how my submission was "scored" but, after 27 years of service, I was credited with 8 years and 5 months for enhanced leave purposes, which allows me to earn leave at the rate of 6 hours/pay period. Again, I chalked this up as a "win" (19.5 days/year as opposed to 13) and moved on. I suggest you provide all of your particular information and let the HR Team apply their calculus to your request and see what results of it.

One more item regarding leave. If you're a 30 percent or more disabled veteran, you should also request **Disabled Veteran's Leave. Many of my peers, now civil servants, had never even heard of this benefit – and it's an entitlement (not discretionary) so don't forget to ask!**

"Under the Wounded Warriors Federal Leave Act of 2015 (Public Law 114-75, November 5, 2015), an employee hired on or after November 5, 2016, who is a veteran with a service-connected disability rating of 30 percent or more from the Veterans Benefits Administration (VBA) of the Department of Veterans Affairs is entitled to up to 104 hours of disabled veteran leave for the purposes of undergoing medical treatment for such disability."

Disabled Veteran's Leave allows a newly hired disabled veteran to join the civil service with some credit for leave to attend to medical appointments, rehabilitation or therapy required as a result of their VA recognized disability or condition. This equates to 4 hours (or ½ a day) per pay period, and expires after 12 months of federal service.

OPM explains it in more detail, here: https://www.opm.gov/policy-data-oversight/pay-leave/leave-administration/fact-sheets/disabled-veteran-leave/

And lastly, upon receipt of the TJO, you should consider requesting any relocation incentives that you may be entitled to. The decision-making authority is almost always the Agency Director (in D.C.) and that may delay your hiring. (Hint: At the time of my hiring, I was told that the Department of the Navy was not currently authorizing any relocation incentives.) But if you think you can make the case, it may be worth asking.

OPM layouts the policies for relocation incentives here: https://www.opm.gov/policy-data-oversight/pay-leave/recruitment-relocation-retention-incentives/fact-sheets/relocation-incentives/

ONE FINAL NOTE: Don't request Property Management fees or reimbursement for Real Estate fees on your initial assignment. Newly hired government employees on their initial assignment are not entitled to Property Management or Real Estate fees, so save your time. GSA spells it out very well, here: https://www.gsa.gov/policy-regulations/regulations/federal-travel-regulation-ftr/i1183555

Example: Superior Qualifications Request Memo

Date: _________________

From: Insert your name here, Prospective Hire for (insert Position Title here), (GS##), ABC Command

To: Human Resource Office, ABC Command

Subject: SUPERIOR QUALIFICATIONS JUSTIFICATION

1. BLUF: This memo is to provide justification of my superior qualifications to substantiate my request for a step increase to GS-## Step #, at $ 98,765.00

2. In this position, I will serve as the as (insert Position Title here) for the ABC Command, where I will (insert brief description, what will you do?).

3. In order to do this effectively, I bring the following specialized skills:

    A. Previous experience in coordinating….. This role provides me unique insights, as well as current points of contacts and other service staffs to ensure alignment. For my efforts in this role, I was recognized by ….

    B. Recent experience working in this environment. Upon my departure I was submitted for a ______ Award (pending.)

    C. Industry specific experience, having worked … At the conclusion of my tour, I was awarded the _________ Medal in recognition of my contributions…

4. While the education requirement listed is for a bachelor's degree, I hold the following degrees or other certificates: List any/all educational experience – especially above/beyond what the position requires.

5. My former employment was with (list company), as a (insert current/former position/ title). In that role I was paid an annual salary of $ 98,765. This request for GS-XX, Step # is intended to meet that rate. (see supporting contract and/or final pay slip, attached.)

6. In conclusion, I hope that you will find sufficient justification for my requested step increase to a GS-XX, Step #. Should you need any additional information, please email me at (insert email) or phone me at (insert phone).

Respectfully submitted,

(Your name & signature here)

Attach: DD214, Previous pay stub, LES, Awards, Education, etc.

Example: Enhanced Leave Request Memo

Date: ______________

FROM: YOUR NAME HERE, prospective INSERT POSITION TITLE (GS-XX)

TO: HRO, HR Specialist, ABC Command

SUBJ: REQUEST FOR ENHANCED LEAVE BASED UPON CREDITABLE SERVICE

1. **BLUF:** This memo is my request for Enhanced Annual Leave based upon creditable uniformed service; my participation in various military campaigns and expeditions as well as my prior active duty roles/responsibilities which directly relate to my pending position. I respect-fully request credit for my prior service in order to earn/accrue leave at the rate of 8 hours per pay period.

2. This request for Enhanced Annual Leave is based upon my accumulation of Creditable Service as defined in Section 6303 of title 5, United States Code and the 2008 National Defense Authorization Act, Section 1115. This memo is broken down for justification purposes into serval sections below: Creditable Uniformed Service (Campaigns and Expeditions); Service Creditable Civilian Service (employment as US Personal Services Contractor); and Creditable Federal Service (US Naval Academy); and Creditable Active Duty Uniformed Service (periods in which my duties/responsibilities directly relate to the position.)

a. Creditable Uniformed Service.

Creditable Uniformed Service is limited to service in the armed forces during a war or in a campaign or expedition for which a campaign badge has been authorized (see DD-214, attached):

Reason	Start	End	Total time
GWOT Expeditionary Medal	09/11/2001	05/30/2018	16 yrs 8 month
GWOT Service Medal	09/11/2001	05/30/2018	16 yrs 8 month
Operation Iraqi Freedom (OIF)	07/01/2004	10/30/2004	0 yrs 4 month
Operation Enduring Freedom (OEF)	12/13/1995	04/03/1996	0 yrs 3 month
NATO Medal (Libya)	03/23/2011	10/31/2011	0 yrs 7 month

National Defense Service Medal (2 Awards)
Armed Forces Expeditionary (3 Awards)

b. Creditable Civilian Service.

Service as a civilian employee, that is, service under a Federal appointment performing Federal functions under Federal supervision (see Contract attached):

Reason	Start	End	Total time
US Personal Services Contractor	11/05/2018	04/19/2020	1 yr 5 month

c. Creditable Federal Service:

2008 National Defense Authorization Act. Section 1115
SEC. 1115. RETIREMENT SERVICE CREDIT FOR SERVICE AS CADET OR MIDSHIPMAN AT A MILITARY SERVICE ACADEMY. Amends Section 8331(13) and Section 8401(31) of title 5, United States Code, to ensure retirement service credit for service as a cadet or midshipman at a military service academy.

Reason	Start	End	Total time
US Naval Academy	07/01/1987	05/28/1991	3 yrs 11 month

(prior federal service, noted on my DD-214 however, this time is not included in my retirement and should therefore be creditable here for leave purposes.)

d. Creditable Active Duty Uniformed Service:

Prior non-Federal Service or Active Duty Uniformed Service that otherwise would not be creditable having duties which directly relate to the duties of the position to which appointed and are necessary to achieve an important agency mission or performance goal, according to Section 6303(e) of title 5, United States Code, as amended by section 202(a) of the Federal Workforce Flexibility Act of 2004 (Document such service credit on the SF-144A):

Active Duty Assignment	Start	End	Total time
OPNAV Staff	Aug 1998	Aug 2001	3 yrs 0 month
NATO Defense College	July 2009	Feb 2010	0 yrs 7 month
NATO Maritime Command	Feb 2010	1 July 2013	3 yrs 5 month
C6F Staff	July 2013	July 2015	2 yrs 0 month
CNO Staff	July 2015	July 2018	3 yrs 0 month

Specific duties which directly relate to this (insert title) position:

    A. List specific, concrete and measurable knowledge, skills and abilities which you learned during your military service.

    B. List only those skills that can be directly linked to your position.

3. I believe the above stated periods more than substantiate my prior creditable service exceeding 15 years which should allow me to accrue leave at the rate of 8 hours per pay period; however, failing to meet that goal, my service in military campaigns and with USAID should more meet the threshold for earning leave at the rate of 6 hours per period.

4. Should you require any additional information, please do not hesitate to contact me at: (insert email here) or (insert phone number here).

                              Respectfully submitted,

                              (Your name & signature here)

Chapter 6

"What to expect while you're expecting… your Final Job Offer."

After acceptance of your TJO, you may have some time waiting for the process to play out. You will have some tasks but they are often sporadic and like most everything else, conducted completely in serial. Most important among those steps will be:

1. **Urinalysis –** ordered by the Hiring Agency HRO and tasked out to a local provider in your area. You may have to set up an appointment, or some may allow walk-ins. Important to note: once issued, you must complete the urinalysis within the set timeframe, so confirm with your HRO before it is issued, especially if you may be out of town or otherwise unavailable to complete it. Secondly, the paperwork they give you is important! It establishes the chain of custody and confirms you completed it on time. Do not lose it. I recommend you take a photo and email it to your HRO.

2. **Physical Examination –** this should also be ordered by your Hiring Agency HRO; however, they may expect that you will know how and where to get this done, usually at a Military Facility which is familiar with Civil Service hiring practices. You may need to do some research for your area. (Hint: This isn't the same as your VA physical. Don't ask a lot of questions or complain…**be truthful, but don't volunteer any information that isn't required.**) The results are normally sent directly back to your HRO. This sounds simple, but since you will not handle any of the paperwork yourself, you will need to ensure connectivity between the medical staff and HRO to verify that they complete the appropriate forms. Some positions may not require a physical.

3. **Security Clearance –** this will be handled by the Hiring Agency's SSO, or Special Security Office. Ordinarily, you will know this is a requirement from the position description or job announcement. As a veteran, you've likely to have played this game before; however, depending upon how long it's been since your last review/adjudication, the rules of the game may have changed completely. For the latest information, guides and instructions go here: https://nbib.opm.gov/e-qip-background-investigations/

Your first step will be an email notification which reads:

> "Dear User,
>
> The following unique e-QIP Registration Code has been automatically generated for your use in establishing your account in the Electronic Questionnaires for Investigations Processing (e-QIP) system. e-QIP is the application System for background investigations and reinvestigations. You will receive a separate communication from your sponsoring agency with instructions on the utilization of this Registration Code for establishing your e-QIP account."

Once you activate your e-Qip account, you will receive a second email which provides a user guide and instructions for entering your information, but also warns:

> ****Log in within 7 calendar days and complete your e-QIP form within 14 calendar days (excluding Federal holidays), or this investigation request may be terminated.****

I hope that you will be pleasantly surprised to discover that your previous information has been saved in the e-QIP system, and you now only need to modify or update it with the latest details. Be sure that you understand the time periods covered, usually 10 years. Again, don't provide information beyond what is requested. (Hint: For foreign travel, Facebook may remember better than you!)

Regarding foreign contacts, you need to understand the following definition:

*"**A foreign national** is defined as **any person who is not a citizen or national of the U.S. You must indicate whether you have, or have had,** close and/or continuing contact **with a foreign national within the last seven years with whom you, or your spouse, or legally recognized civil union/ domestic partner, or cohabitant** are bound by affection, influence, common interests, and/or obligation."*

If you do find yourself starting your e-Qip entries from scratch, I suggest you do so with the most recent copy of your credit report handy, as it will know all of your history and previous addresses. You will also need the point of contact information for family, friends, neighbors and associates who can vouch for you at each of your previous addresses and employers. These references will need to be U.S. Citizens currently residing in the U.S. to satisfy requirements.

This can be laborious… start early and get it submitted on-time. The eQip system will automatically lock you out, either when you hit submit or in 14-days. If you need additional time, communicate that immediately to the SSO.

There is a way to save a copy of your submission, either by printing or selecting print and then "save as a .pdf" and I suggest that you do this before submitting your information.

4. **Fingerprinting –** You may be required to submit your fingerprints. This is now done electronically, so you will need access to a base or military facility. Your servicing HRO should be able to recommend one, but may be complicated if you are not located near a military base.

Chapter 7

"Receipt/ Acceptance of your Final Job Offer."

Upon receipt of your Final Job Offer or "FJO"[4] you'll once again be directed to the USA Jobs onboarding website to accept the offer. However, before doing so, be sure to re-read the FJO thoroughly (see example page 41).

Specifically, you will want to ensure that you agree with and understand:

1. **The Position Title** – again, it may sound petty, but ensure this is the exact position you applied for and previously accepted in the TJO.

2. **The Starting Pay Grade, Step and Salary** – if you have requested and been approved for Superior Qualifications, that should be specifically mentioned.

3. **Entrance On Duty (Eod) Date** – this should be mutually agreed upon and reasonable given your circumstances, location and required travel.

4. **The Length Of Tour** – especially important for overseas positions and managing travel requirements.

5. **Enhanced Leave Accrual** – ensure that your previous request for creditable service time has been addressed and resolved to your satisfaction. This will determine the rate at which you earn leave. (see previous discussion in Chapter 4)

6. **Benefits/Entitlements Allowed Or Denied** – read through these and follow the links provided to OPM if you're uncertain.

7. **Security Clearance** – verify that the requirement listed matches your current/ anticipated level of clearance.

8. **Probationary/Trial Period** – same as previously discussed with TJO.

---

4. Nearly everyone refers to this as simply "the FJO" or "Final Job Offer." However, it in researching this ebook, I have seen it described as: "Final Job Offer," "Final Job Letter," "Official Job Offer" and/or "Official Job Letter." Yet always utilizing the acronym, "FJO."

When you've verified the above information, proceed to the on-boarding portal where you will be given three options: accept the position, decline the position or request additional information. Clearly if you're ready to accept, do so immediately – same if you're moving on to another option and intend to decline. Don't wait. If you're somewhere in-between and have questions, doubts or confusion, email your HRO point of contact immediately <u>and</u> click on the "request additional information" option, BEFORE the offer expires, usually 72 hours.

Bottomline: If you have issues, concerns or questions, communicate early, often and in-writing, before you accept the Final Job Offer.

Example: Final Job Offer (FJO) Letter

Dear (Your name here):

Please go to the following link, respond within 3 business days of this offer, and complete the newly assigned tasks in the USA Staffing New Hire Module, if assigned: https://onboard.usastaffing.gov/?newhire=HO6UP-BKCF&type=official

This letter is an official job offer for the position of INSERT TITLE HERE, GS-0130-XX (full performance level GS- XX) with the OFFICE OF THE COMMANDER located in ABC COMMAND. This offer letter includes the final compensation package (excluding benefits) for this position.

The command has authorized setting your salary at a rate higher than the minimum step of the grade based on your superior qualifications.

Your pay is set at GS-XX, Step 03, $ 98,765.00 per annum.

Note: Locality pay is not authorized overseas; this salary does not include any pay outs, general pay increases or within grade increases the employee may receive prior to the effective date of this action (if applicable).

EOD: This letter serves as the official notification of selection and formal request for release upon the written acceptance of this offer. Upon written acceptance of this offer, we request an Entrance on duty (EOD) date (on or about) of (usually between 2 weeks to 2 months from receipt, if this is an overseas position). However, this on/about date is contingent upon the successful completion of all required pre-employment documents (i.e. physical examination, security background screening, ability to obtain a no-fee official passports, and any other overseas requirements, etc.), as applicable for the country of entry and/or position requirements. Your actual EOD date will be based upon your travel itinerary. For current federal employees, your "losing" HRO should assist you with the coordination of your actual release date, and the official notification to your current organization.

Please note that if your actual travel date is initiated towards the end of the pay period, your first initial pay check may be delayed, due to the short processing timeframes.

Length of Tour: The initial tour length is 36 months.

Official Passport and Visa: Upon written acceptance of this offer, this letter will serve as your authorization to arrange for the preparation of DD-1056, authorization to apply for official passport and/ or visa for you and family members. Specific information on consulates and travel regulations for each country is available at: www.travel.state.gov.

If currently a Federal employee, contact your installation PSD/ Passport Office for assistance with application process. New employees may request assistance from the nearest DoD Human Resources Office. The pre-departure subsistence expense portion of Foreign Transfer Allowance (FTA) is limited to ten days, therefore, until both the passport(s) and visa(s) are received, you may not commence travel to foreign area or move into temporary quarters.

Permanent Change of Station (PCS) orders: PCS orders will be issued by the Overseas Human Resources Office upon receipt of all required documents.

Overseas allowances: General information on overseas allowances is available at: http://www.defensetravel.dod.mil/site/faqpcs.cfm. Requests for more specific information as well as requests for advance salary entitlement are to be directed to the Overseas Human Resources Office.

Shipment of Household Goods and/or Privately Owned Vehicle: Upon receipt of the PCS orders, you may initiate contact with your personal property and transportation office (or one located in the nearest military facility if not a current Federal employee) to make necessary arrangements.

IMPORTANT NOTES:

- Security Clearance Required: This position requires the ability to obtain and maintain a top secret with SCI security clearance. Inability to obtain and maintain the required clearance level may be a cause for removal from the position.

- Advanced Leave Accrual: This appointment includes a service credit towards annual leave accrual rate earned for 8 years, 5 months. This credit remains permanent once you have completed one full year of continuous federal employment.

- Probationary/Trial Period: This appointment is subject to a 2-year probationary period.

GOVERNMENT ETHICS REQUIREMENTS: The Department of the Navy is committed to maintaining an ethical culture and upholding the principles of ethical conduct. As a Department of the Navy employee, you will be subject to the Standards of Ethical Conduct for Employees of the Executive Branch as well as the criminal conflict of interest statutes. If you are a new Government employee, or as a new employee to this Department, you will be required to receive initial ethics orientation within 3 months of appointment. If you have any questions about these requirements, or any government ethics issue, you should contact the ethics counselor for your organization which will be located in your local Counsel or Judge Advocate General's office. If you need assistance locating your local ethics counselor please email ethics@navy.mil.

Additional reporting day information (i.e., reporting date, time, location and map) will be provided. If you have not received this information or if you have questions regarding the electronic completion and submission of forms, please contact (LIST HRO POC INFO).

Note: The reporting date reflected on the PCS orders is approximate and can be changed if the required documents have not been received in a timely manner. Therefore, it is critical that we are notified of your departure date or any delays in receiving the required documents. Since the departure date is the effective date of your personnel action and accession to our rolls, it is imperative that I and your Overseas HRO POC are provided your travel itinerary as soon as one is established. Failure to provide a travel itinerary by email prior to your departure date will result in delays of regular pay, advances, overseas base access, etc.

As a reminder, you must bring the original version of the documents previously submitted as proof of citizenship and identification as failure to exhibit these documents during your in-processing may result in postponement of your employment.

This letter serves as official notification of your selection and must be exhibited at the entrance gate or pass and ID office to gain access to the installation. I wish you the best in your new position.

Sincerely,

HRO Point of Contact

Chapter 8

"Joining the Civil Service."

I participated in an on-line retirement planning seminar for Federal Employees, the FERS Retirement Seminar in Dec 2020. It was hosted by Mr. Lou Garner, of Union Consulting in Virginia. He is both a DoD veteran retiree and a FERS retiree. He was a wealth of knowledge and I highly recommend that if you're able to attend a similar retirement planning seminar, that you do so as soon as possible, as we veterans are older (and closer to retirement) than the average person joining the civil service. Many of the choices you make upon entering the civil service will have an impact on your retirement.

Let's discuss the **Federal Employees Retirement System (FERS).**

"Congress created the FERS in 1986, and it became effective on January 1, 1987. Since that time, new Federal civilian employees who have retirement coverage are covered by FERS.

FERS is a retirement plan that provides benefits from three different sources: a Basic Benefit Plan, Social Security and the Thrift Savings Plan (TSP). Two of the three parts of FERS (Social Security and the TSP) can go with you to your next job if you leave the Federal Government before retirement. The Basic Benefit and Social Security parts of FERS require you to pay your share each pay period. Your agency withholds the cost of the Basic Benefit and Social Security from your pay as payroll deductions. Your agency pays its part too. Then, after you retire, you receive annuity payments each month for the rest of your life." (OPM)

The Basic Benefit or FERS annuity is, like military retirement, based on your average high-3 salary. Generally, the benefit is calculated as 1 percent of high-3 average pay multiplied by years of creditable service. For those retiring at age 62 or later with at least 20 years of service, a factor of 1.1 percent is used rather than 1 percent. OPM provides a host of information regarding FERS and it's worth educating yourself on this important benefit, here: https://www.opm.gov/retirement-services/fers-information/

Now, I would like to highlight a few points and recommendations which relate to veterans joining the civil service, particularly if you are fortunate enough to be a veteran that is receiving an active-duty pension.

As you begin your career as a civil servant, you'll want to understand a few key dates:

- **Your joining date** – normally the day you are sworn in/joined the federal service;

- **Service Computation Date (SCD)** – normally +3 years from joining, this determines the date upon which you will be fully vested in TSP and eligible to retain your agency's matching contributions (if any);

- **Minimum Retirement Age (MRA)** – age at which you are eligible to retire with FERS.

Military retirees are not likely to remain in the civil service long enough to maximize their FERS retirements. The best advice is to discuss any/all options with your HRO (spouse and financial advisor as well) before deciding anything. However, as an overview, several other options may be available to you regarding your participation in FERS, including:

1. **Opt out** – some positions may allow you to completely opt out of FERS, potentially allowing you to retain the percentage of pay roll contributions that you would otherwise make (not recommended);

2. **Early retirement** – retiring at MRA+10 with a minimum of 5 years of civil service; your retirement annuity will be reduced 5% for each year you retire under age 62, or your full retirement age (not recommended);

3. **Postponed retirement** – Retiring prior to age 62, but electing to defer receipt of your annuity benefits until you reach your full retirement age (RECOMMENDED);

4. **Withdraw** – Request a complete refund of your retirement deductions. This will eliminate your rights to an annuity for the period of service that the refund covers. (not recommended) see: https://www.opm.gov/retirement-services/fers-information/former-employees/ for more details.

Perhaps the best thing that a veteran joining the civil service can do, is to request Creditable Civilian Service to "buy back" military time. Buying back time, will not make sense for 99% of veterans who have retired after 20 years of service with a pension.

The monetary value of your active duty retirement will far exceed the value of buying back 20 years of service and then retiring under FERS with those same years, plus your GS time.

Therefore, this only makes sense to be done for **military time which is not included in your military pension,** such as a reservist, or time spent as a Midshipman or Cadet at a Service Academy. (Full disclosure: I am uncertain how creditable service applies for ROTC.)

There is a great article outlining the process, here: https://www.govloop.com/community/blog/need-know-credit-military-service/

Your first step will be to complete a request for estimated earnings during military service (RI- 20-97), available here: https://www.opm.gov/forms/pdf_fill/Ri20-97.pdf.

Once that is determined, you will need to complete the application to make a federal service credit payment (SF-3108-13), available here: https://www.gsa.gov/cdnstatic/SF3108-13.pdf?forceDownload=1.

Many HR Staff will not be familiar with this process. So, if you intend to do this, I suggest that you talk to your servicing HRO after you've completed your on-boarding process. You should complete this as early as possible in your new career, as you will need to make an equitable contribution (adjusted for inflation) to your FERS in order to "buy back" those years. If you're able to complete your full contribution to FERS within your initial years of civil service, you may not accrue any additional interest.

A note or two for FERS planning:

- FERS has a survivorship benefit (akin to Survivor's Benefit Plan, SBP, for your Active Duty pension). This will reduce your FERS pension by 10% and will provide your surviving spouse with 50% of your benefit. There is an excellent and short article, here for your consideration: https://www.federaldisability.com/blog/2018/02/fers-survivor-benefits-should-elect/#share. **(Hint: Consider waiving this benefit and retaining you full FERS annuity, especially if you already have the Survivor's Benefit Plan.)**

- The best date to retire is the end of the month and the end of the year. OPM and/or Google will tell you which days are best. You can also check other websites, such as: https://www.myfederalretirement.com/best-dates-retire/ (Hint: I recommend that you also subscribe to their emails for great info on FERS and TSP.)

- OPM may take 6 months or more to calculate your retirement benefits.

Thrift Savings Plan (TSP). TSP was originally only for Federal civilian employees, however in 2001, the National Defense Authorization Act extended participation to members of the uniformed services. So, hopefully, many of you are already familiar with this benefit.

The TSP is the Federal Government's 401K, or tax deferred savings plan, for federal employees. It has one of the lowest expense ratios available anywhere, currently at 0.060% (or less). Another way of saying that is that TSP participants' investments were reduced by 60 cents for every $1,000 invested. The TSP has a very educational website here: https://www.tsp.gov/

Matching contributions. The good news is that in the civil service, **"the USG provides matching contributions on the first 5% of pay that you contribute each pay period.**

Your Biweekly Contribution	Automatic 1% Contribution	Agency Matching Contribution	Total Contributions
0%	1%	0%	1%
1%	1%	1%	3%
2%	1%	2%	5%
3%	1%	3%	7%
4%	1%	3.5%	8.5%
5%	1%	4%	10%
5% +	1%	4%	Your % + 5%

The first 3% of pay that you contribute will be matched dollar-for-dollar; the next 2% will be matched at 50 cents on the dollar. Contributions above 5% of your pay will not be matched. If you stop making regular employee contributions, your matching contributions will also stop."

https://www.tsp.gov/making-contributions/contribution-types/

You should understand the funds available for your TSP contributions and decide how you would like to allocate your contributions each month. TSP currently offers the following:

- G Fund, or Government Securities Investment fund. Designed to produce a rate of return higher than inflation while avoiding exposure to credit (default) risk.

- F Fund, or Fixed Income Index Investment fund. Designed to match the performance of the Bloomberg Barclays U.S. Aggregate Bond Index.

- C Fund, or Common Stock Index Investment fund. Designed to match the performance of the Standard and Poor's 500 (S&P 500) Index.

- S Fund, or Small Cap Stock Index Investment fund. Designed to match the performance of the Dow Jones U.S. Completion Total Stock Market Index.

- I Fund, or International Stock Index Investment fund. Designed to match the performance of the MSCI EAFE (Europe, Australasia, Far East) Index.

- L Funds, or Lifecycle (L) funds. Each of the ten different L Funds is a diversified mix of the core funds (G, F, C, S, and I), designed to provide the best expected return for an appropriate level of risk, determined by your selected retirement date.

There are some caveats on TSP:

- Your TSP may lose money; see: https://www.tsp.gov/fund-performance/

- You must make contributions throughout the year – all 26 pay periods – in order to be eligible to receive USG matching contributions.

- You need to serve for a minimum of 3 years to become "vested" with your matching contributions; should you leave government service before 3 years, you risk losing your matching contributions.

- You may be able to transfer other eligible retirement savings (i.e., a 401K) into your TSP. **(Hint: compare your 401K expense ratio and any fees with TSP's rate of 0.060%.)**

Social Security is the third leg of your FERS retirement plan. I'm not going to discuss it here, other than to suggest:

- An annual review of your Social Security Statement (and you can log-in and get one today at: https://secure.ssa.gov/RIL/SiView.action) to verify all of your wages have been included in their calculations.

- A review of the information contained within the Military Service and Social Security pamphlet, here: https://www.ssa.gov/pubs/EN-05-10017.pdf.

- Know that, as of today, neither your military retirement nor your FERS retirement will have any impact upon your eligibility to receive Social Security.

A brief note on the Federal Employees Health Benefit Plan (FEHB) and Federal Employee Group Life Insurance (FEGLI).

The Federal Employees Health Benefit (FEHB) is probably not worth the expense for military retirees currently covered by Tricare; however, as you near your FERS retirement date, it's likely worth joining, in order to have an active FEHB on the last day/week/month prior to your retirement. Having an active FEHB policy on the day of your retirement from FERS will ensure that you are eligible to re-start it later (and pay for it) should you ever need to do so.

Assuming that you have left work before age 62, and that you are deferring your FERS retirement, you can also defer/suspend your FEHB healthcare… that way when Tricare puts you on Medicare (at age 62), you could re-activate FEHB. Of course, that means that you will have to pay for it; however, it's worth noting that the USG pays 75% you pay "only" 25%.

Regardless of your intentions now, I recommend you re-visit FEHB prior to your FERS retirement. There article will help ensure that you meet the requirements: https://www.myfederalretirement.com/fehb-retirement/

The Federal Employee Group Life Insurance (FEGLI) is another benefit offered, and at first glance may appear wonderful, as the Federal Government pays one-third of the cost of your Basic level of life insurance; however, it may not be the best deal available to you.

If you are healthy and otherwise eligible, it's recommended that you shop for other life insurance. If you don't already have a policy, I suggest you request some quotes from some of the many service-oriented providers, such as Navy Mutual Aid, WAEPA, USAA - or even VGLI, if you're still eligible. Again, just my thoughts (not financial or investing guidance): shop around and see what's best for you and your family. You may find a better deal than FEGLI offers.

If you decide to retain FEGLI, take some time to understand the 3 other levels of coverage offered, beyond Basic: https://www.opm.gov/healthcare-insurance/life-insurance/. There are even links to some useful Youtube videos. Be sure that you understand (and compare) the costs associated with the different levels of FEGLI coverage offered. There is a useful calculator available here: https://www.opm.gov/retirement-services/calculators/fegli-calculator/.

Upon joining, you may be asked to complete a Life Insurance Election Form, or SF-2817, available here: https://www.opm.gov/forms/pdf_fill/sf2817.pdf. This form is also used to cancel or decline your FEGLI; however, your HRO may require you to show that you have other life insurance already in-place, so bring a copy of your policy with you when on-boarding.

Chapter 9
"Avoiding Possible Pitfalls"

Throughout the process and research for this ebook, as well as having lived vicariously through my wife's 10+ year civil service career, I have managed to identify a few areas of concern.

Excepted Service: the focus of this ebook is on positions within the competitive service. Ensure that you know exactly the type for which you are applying. Term hire positions have an expiry date and do not qualify you for the competitive service. Having said that, Veterans preference may still allow you to apply for follow on positions, and accepting a term position may give you a 'foot in the door' for competitive positions that later open up in the workplace. The difference between excepted and competitive service may be as simple as a coded entry (in Box 34 on your SF-50 employment record) 1 for competitive service and 2 for excepted service. After on-boarding, verify that your position is properly coded and ensure that you understand any limitations if you accept a position in the excepted service.

Spouse Hire: Similar to the above, many spouse hires, grateful to have gained meaningful employment, don't realize that their status in the excepted service will have significant impacts which last beyond their current assignment. Even if they apply for and win a position competitively, spouses hired overseas are usually considered local hires, and placed in the 'excepted service' (code 2 in Box 34 in the SF-50) with an 'indefinite term' (code 3 in Box 24 of the SF-50). The term is tied to their spouse's orders. Again if you accept a position such as this, be sure you understand the immediate and long-term implications. You may not have 'return rights' to a US position, cannot apply for positions in the competitive service (unless they are open to current military spouses) and may have difficulty accessing the Priority Placement Program (PPP).

The PPP is a program that offers placement assistance to allow DoD civilians to continue their careers, following a move or Reduction in Force. The DoD Instruction for PPP is here: https://www.dcpas.osd.mil/Content/documents/OD/PPPHandbook.pdf However, it's not very user friendly. An easy-to-read guide for employees is available, here: https://dma.wi.gov/DMA/hr/placement/helppamphlet.pdf.

Lastly, if serving overseas, spouse hires are not entitled to allowances or privileges, other than base pay.

Overseas Allowances and Differentials: are not automatic salary supplements, nor are they entitlements. They are specifically intended to be recruitment incentives for U.S. citizen civilian employees living in the United States to accept Federal employment in a foreign area. If a person is already living in the foreign area, that inducement is normally unnecessary.

You are <u>not</u> automatically granted overseas allowances and benefits because you may meet the eligibility requirements. This is particularly true if you should decide to extend overseas… there are some who will misinterpret your willingness to remain overseas as a signal that these additional benefits are no longer required to retain your services (remember they were offered originally as 'recruitment incentives').

Living Quarters Allowance (LQA): is the civilian equivalent to active duty Variable Housing Allowance (VHA), with one significant difference: for civilians, this benefit is offered at the command's discretion. In 27 years of active duty, I don't' recall anyone ever having been denied VHA (Overseas) or Basic Allowance for Housing (CONUS). However, I know several civilians who have run afoul of the LQA rules and policy (mis)interpretations of the LQA granting authorities.

In all fairness, it wasn't that many years ago when there was a major misinterpretation of the rules, that caused many civilians to be overpaid in Germany. You can read all about it here: https://www.stripes.com/news/error-could-force-civilian-employees-in-europe-to-repay-housing-allowances-1.193274. Therefore, it's understandable that HRO, and the lawyers who support them, are overly cautious.

Upon hiring, your servicing Human Resources Office will ask you to complete an LQA questionnaire in order to determine your eligibility. THIS IS VERY IMPORTANT. They will be looking to determine that you have been "resident in the Continental United States for the entirety of the recruitment period." That means you were physically located within the United States, 100% of the time from submitting your application to on-boarding. They will ask you to provide copies each and every page in your passport(s) as proof.

There are some exceptions, but trust me when I tell you, LQA entitlements are not something you should trifle with. Accepting a position overseas without LQA may cost you $50,000 a year or more in living expenses, alone. Plus, if you are not granted LQA, you may not be eligible for other related allowances (such as TQSA, see below) and services, such as assistance from housing for inspections, contracting or negotiating landlord disputes.

LQA eligibility exceptions may be granted for existing civil servants applying for a new position while already serving abroad. If you are currently serving abroad, or intend to retire from active duty while serving abroad you need to be very careful. You should <u>not</u> execute any portion of your return/transportation agreement to the U.S. during the recruitment period or you may be found ineligible for LQA. Talk with your HRO (and perhaps the legal advisor) as early as possible in your hiring process.

Temporary Quarters Subsistence Allowance (TQSA): is a non-taxable supplement for employees traveling to/from an overseas duty location on official travel orders and authorized Living Quarters Allowance. This allowance covers expenses for lodging, meals, laundry and dry cleaning not to exceed maximum allowance. TQSA is granted for up to 90 days (in 30 day increments) after your arrival at the overseas duty station. (For your standard PCS move, this can easily add up to $3,000 per month or more.)

The Department of State website, with helpful FAQs and other, source information, is here: https://aoprals.state.gov/content.asp?content_id=160&menu_id=75

DOD has its own FAQs for the implementation of the Dept. Of State LQA regulations outlined here: https://www.defensetravel.dod.mil/site/faqlqa.cfm

LQA and TQSA: Ensure that you are and remain within the Continental United States throughout your recruiting period. If you intend to leave the United States (or where you are currently assigned) even for a vacation, be sure that you coordinate with your servicing HRO and understand this may put your LQA and TQSA benefits at-risk.

Active Duty Retirement from Overseas: Don't. There have been several people who have retired from active duty while serving overseas and later, when seeking subsequent employment with the federal government overseas, they were refused LQA. The logic being that since these individuals retired while overseas, they clearly don't require any 'recruitment incentive' to accept another position overseas. This is despite the fact that one person had retired from active duty in Japan and was seeking a position in Europe. If you're on active duty and intend to retire from abroad, I have one piece of advice: Don't do it! Return to CONUS and be retire/out-process from within the continental U.S.A.

LQA and Dual Working Couples: Ordinarily one Civilian employee, at the Civilian employee's option, may receive the basic 'with family' allowance rate plus increments for additional family members. The other Civilian employee may receive the 'without family' rate. If there are no additional family members, each Civilian employee may receive the 'without family' rate. (This is generally also true if one is active duty instead of another civil servant.) See additional information here: https://www.defensetravel.dod.mil/site/faqdual.cfm

HR Staff may "for simplicity's sake" or "because that's how we've always handled these dual cases," assume to know your desires and consolidate your family into a single set of entitlements, or on a single set of orders. Be sure that you understand how you and your spouse will be assigned and how LQA is calculated, so that you can make an informed decision on which set of orders you should place your dependents. Do your research here:

https://www.defensetravel.dod.mil/site/faqlqa.cfm. (Hint: If you are in this unique and fortunate position, be proactive and communicate your intentions to the servicing HRO early and in-writing. Since one LQA will be 'with family' and the other 'without', I suggest all dependents should be on the 'with family' orders, as you generally receive an additional amount (10%) for subsequent family members.)

Taxes: As a result of the 2017 Tax Cuts and Jobs Act, many Civilian PCS Allowances are now taxable (unlike active duty or the foreign service). LQA and Post Allowance are not taxable; however, the following list of special pays/allowance may be taxed:

- Certain repairs to a leased home;

- Education of dependents in special situations;

- POV shipment (taxed in CONUS, not taxed to/from overseas);

- Separate maintenance for dependents;

- Temporary quarters expenses;

- Travel, moving, and storage expenses.

The IRS provides some helpful information here: https://www.irs.gov/individuals/international-taxpayers/allowances-differentials-and-other-special-pay and https://www.irs.gov/pub/irs-pdf/p516.pdf.

When conducting a Permanent Change of Station (PCS) move as a civilian in the DoD, it will be difficult to control your costs. This can be frustrating because ultimately you will be responsible for 1/3 of the travel expenses, in taxes. The DoD will arrange your flights and often mandates where you can stay (Air B&B is not allowed) and then, when the reimbursement for travel claim comes through, it will only refund 2/3 of the total. So, you are likely to incur out-of-pocket expenses to complete your PCS move. At the end of the year, you will receive a separate Travel W-2 that accounts for your PCS expenses (including any moving and storage fees incurred) and applicable taxes withheld.

When conducting an overseas PCS, you should be eligible for Foreign Transfer Allowances. The Miscellaneous Expense Allowance (MEA) is a one-time payment to defray some of the costs incurred, and is usually $750 (single) or $1500 (with family.) There is also a way to request an up-front allowance to address your anticipated taxes, called the Withholding Tax Allowance. It is specifically intended to help you avoid out-of-pocket expenses when paying the taxes owed on your PCS move. However, if you choose to pay the taxes, you can request a refund through the Defense Financial Accounting Service (DFAS), called the Relocation Income Tax Allowance (RITA). If you apply for the WTA, you must submit a RITA claim. If the RITA claim is less than the WTA, you will owe a debt to DFAS. The reimbursement you receive will be taxable.

Don't underestimate the costs of moving, in my case, during our recent overseas move (for a family of four) they were over $20,000, with $4,500 paid in taxes.

However, in full disclosure I have not completed the RITA process yet. (Hint: RITA is new and the process seems overly involved. For example: You will be asked to submit a copy of your tax-return and if you have filed a joint tax return, your RITA claim also requires the signature of your spouse.)

The Defense Finance and Accounting System (DFAS) provides a wealth of information, including specifics on WTA and RITA, here: https://www.dfas.mil/CivilianEmployees/Civilian-Permanent-Change-of-Station-PCS/Civilian-PCS-Entitlement-Guide/Relocation-Income-Tax-Allowance-RITA/

Action checklist

Chapter 1: Planning and Preparing

- Verify your veteran's preference using Dept of Labor website
- Apply for disability from Veteran's Administration
- Create a USA Jobs account – walk through job application
- Verify your email and mobile phone will meet requirements

Chapter 2: Finding and Applying

- Create your federal resume, using Ms. Troutman's book
- Complete your SF-15 for Veteran's Preference
- Upload required documents to USA Jobs profile
- Set up USA Jobs search(es)
- Update your Social Media profile, Facebook and Linked In (Google yourself)
- Identify Veteran's Hiring Council Representative for desired agencies
- Rehearse 6-8 scenario-based answers in S-T-A-R Format
- Conduct at least 1 practice interview in-person
- Ensure you're familiar with Zoom and Microsoft teams

Chapter 3: The Hiring Process

- Keep your day job!

Chapter 4: Receipt of your Tentative Job Offer (TJO)

- Re-read and verify all elements of your TJO
- Communicate any questions and/or concerns - immediately
- Respond before the TJO deadline
- Complete any onboarding forms carefully – they determine your allowances!

Chapter 5: Maintaining your options upon acceptance of your Tentative Job Offer (TJO)

- Keep your options open – seek other employment
- Submit memorandum for "Superior Qualifications"
- Submit memorandum and SG-144A for "Enhanced Leave" consideration
- Submit request for Disabled Veteran's Leave (if entitled)
- Submit request for any relocation incentive(s)

Chapter 6: What to expect when you're expecting… your Final Job Offer (FJO)

- Complete urinalysis: keep paperwork, email HRO a copy, ASAP
- Complete physical exam
- Update Security Clearance (as required) using e-Qip, save a copy
- Submit fingerprints (if required)

Chapter 7: Receipt/Acceptance of your Final Job Offer (FJO)

- Re-read and verify all elements of your FJO
- Communicate any questions and concerns - immediately
- Respond before the FJO deadline

Chapter 8: Joining the Civil Service

- Educate yourself on FERS
- Ensure you understand key FERS dates: Joining, SCD and MRA
- Explore FERS options: Opt-out, early, post-pone, withdraw
- Submit Request for "Creditable Civilian Service"

    ✓ Submit RI-20-97, request for Estimated Earnings
    ✓ Submit SF-3108-13, application to make federal service credit payment

- Establish your "new" civilian TSP Account

    ✓ Ensure your contributions span all 26 pay periods (for USG matching)
    ✓ Select appropriate TSP funds for your allocations: C, F, G, I, S or Life Cycle
    ✓ Consider transferring other 401K funds into TSP

- Verify your Annual Social Security Statement
- Determine your medical insurance needs, then accept or decline FEHB
- Determine your life insurance needs, then accept or decline FEGLI

Chapter 9: Avoiding Possible Pitfalls

- Verify if your position is Competitive or Excepted Service
- Spouse Hire categorization and possible impacts
- Overseas Allowances and Differentials
- Remain in the U.S. to preserve eligibility for Living Quarters Allowance (LQA)
- Do NOT retire from Active Duty while Overseas
- LQA and Dual Working Couple concerns
- Beware of Tax implications
- Understanding WTA and RITA